Breaking the Fever

ALSO BY MARY MACKEY

Poetry

Split Ends
Skin Deep
One Night Stand
The Dear Dance of Eros

Novels

Immersion
McCarthy's List
The Last Warrior Queen
A Grand Passion
The Kindness of Strangers
Season of Shadows
The Year The Horses Came
The Horses At the Gate
The Fires of Spring

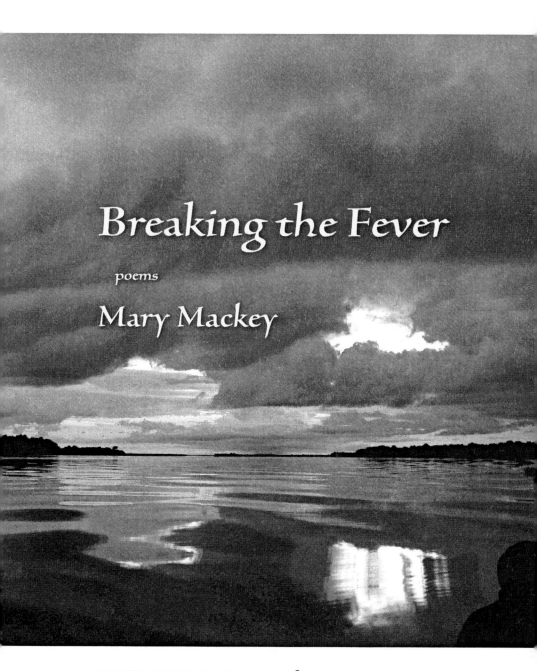

Breaking the Fever

poems

Mary Mackey

MARSH HAWK PRESS · 2006

06 07 08 7 6 5 4 3 2 1 FIRST EDITION

Marsh Hawk Press books are published by Poetry Mailing List, Inc.,
a not-for-profit corporation under section 501 (c) 3 United States
Internal Revenue Code.

Book and cover design: Claudia Carlson
Author photograph, "Amazon Blue" (title page) and "Baja Abstract" (part title pages):
Angus Wright

The text of this book is Adobe Jenson Pro and the display is Adobe Silentium Pro.

Library of Congress Cataloging-in-Publication Data

Mackey, Mary.
  Breaking the fever / Mary Mackey.
    p. cm.
  ISBN-13: 978-0-9724785-8-8 (pbk.)
  ISBN-10: 0-9724785-8-2 (pbk.)
  I. Title.
  PS3563.A3165B74 2006
  813'.54—dc22

                        2006009912

MARSH HAWK PRESS
P.O. Box 206
East Rockaway, New York 11518-0206
www.marshhawkpress.org

Acknowledgments

I would like to thank the Virginia Center for the Creative Arts for awarding me two fellowships which allowed me to create and revise these poems while in residence. Janice Eidus's editorial suggestions were invaluable as were those of Tom Fink and Rochelle Ratner. The photograph, "Amazon Blue," on the cover of this book was created by Angus Wright.

Some of these poems were previously published in the following magazines and anthologies:

Women Poet: The West II: "Lucille"
Yellow Silk: "Blue"; "Instructions for Wrestling with Angels"; "My Methodist Grandmother Said".
Pillow: A Yellow Silk Book: "Don't Start Something You Can't Finish"
WeMoon: "Ex Voto"
Poetry USA: "Breaking the Fever"
Switched-On Gutenberg: A Global Poetry Journal: "The Breakfast Nook";
The Land Report: "Turkeys"; "The Grower of Tomatoes"
Poetry Now: "Netsurfing 2:00 A.M."; "The Visit"; "Not Like We Knew the Answer"; "Samba"
In Sublette's Barn: "Mongoosecivique"
Bay Crossings: "L. Tells All"
So Luminous The Wildflowers: Tebot Bach Anthology of California Poetry: "Clutter"
SacramentoPoetryCenter.org: "Whole Note"; "Memories of My Own Underdevelopment"

for A.W.

Contents

Part 1: The Fever Children   3

Breaking the Fever   5
Chicken Killing   8
First Grade   10
Hit and Run   12
Turkeys   14
L. Tells All   16
My Methodist Grandmother Said   18
Crossing the Lake   21

Part 2: The Californian   23

Memories of My Own Underdevelopment   25
Citizen of Nowhere   27
The Californian   29
Solo   31
The Breakfast Nook   32
Santa Teresa Calls Him (But He Does Not Answer)   34
Mongoosecivique   35
Rumor Had It We Were Eating Dogs   37
Anza-Borrego   39
The Mayans Take Back Yucatan   40
Atlas   43
Peninsula de Osa   44
The Photographer Longs for Something
   She Can't Define   45
Witness   46
The Freedom of High Places   49
Greenhouse   51
Agapanthus   52
Sycamores   54

Part 3: When We Were Your Age   55

When We Were Your Age   57
Not Like We Knew the Answer   60
You Are Making Important Decisions   62
Instructions for Wrestling with Angels   65
Starting Over   68
Lynchburg   69
Walking the Neighborhood   73
Samba   74
Clutter   77
Whole Note   79
Net Surfing 2:00 A.M.   80

Part 4: Another Piece of Kansas   83

Replays   85
Poem for Calling Back the Dead   87
Don't Start Something You Can't Finish   88
Lucille   91
Blue   93
Ex Voto   96
Every Day I Lose Another Piece of Kansas   98
The Grower of Tomatoes   100
The Kama Sutra of Kindness: Position Number 3   101
Missing Your Mouth   104
The Visit   105
Fishing and Weaving   106

Notes   107
About the Author   109

Breaking the Fever

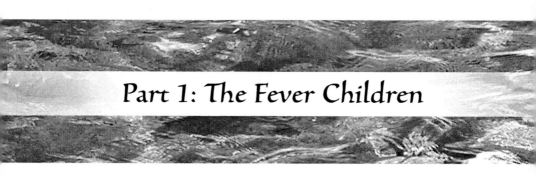

Part 1: The Fever Children

Breaking the Fever

When I was young
fevers were attacked
the grown-ups would rub you
with alcohol
wrap you in wet sheets
refuse you blankets
fan you, feed you aspirin
plunge your wrists in cold water

they knew fever had to be fought
because it let children see
forbidden things
At 105 I would start to hear voices
soft and lulling
at 106 the faces would appear
swimming around me

stretching out their hands
they would gesture to me
to join them
I was always very happy then
floating out on the warm brink
of the world

the fever children
would sing in high voices
liquid like silver bells
come with us
they would say
come play, Mary
and they would show me
maple trees turning red and gold

long aisles of sunlight
and woods that glowed and trembled

My body would start to come apart
very gently like milkweed fluff
and I would begin
to rise up toward their
hands
but always at the last moment
the dark circles
of the grown-ups' faces
would force me back down
and their fear would pin my chest
to the mattress
like black crystal paper weights

They would force more aspirin on me
more ice and alcohol rubs
more wet sheets
and if that didn't work
they would lift my naked body
and plunge it into a tub of cold water
ignoring my screams

Come back
they would plead
come back
come back
and my fever would buckle
and snap like the spine
of a beautiful snake
crushed under a boot

Then the fever children
would abandon me
and I would be left in a world
of ordinary things:
light bulbs
used Kleenex
hissing radiators
thermometers

I would see my mother's pale
terrified face
and my stuffed animals
and my brother's crib
and my precious fever would lie
broken in a thousand bits
with no way to put it back together
and I could never explain
how kind it had been
and how foolish we were to fear it

Chicken Killing

I was 5 and the chickens were my friends

I would pull an ear of corn from the crib
hack it against a brick and cry *here biddy biddy biddy*

and they'd come running to peck between my bare
toes with beaks hard and smooth as sanded oak

when the crabapples rotted and fell off the tree into the yard
they would gobble them up and get drunk

then dance the crabapple dance   cluck
and strut, bump into each other, fly into the side

of the henhouse and stagger around laughing at chicken jokes

I laughed at their jokes   I partied
hard with those hens

one afternoon when we got back from
Hebron Baptist Church where you got to fan yourself
with funeral parlor fans

Uncle Wid went to the chicken yard with an ear
of corn   *here biddy biddy biddy*   he cried

and when the chickens ran up to peck
he grabbed two by the neck and swung them

over his head like sacks   wap   wap   and their heads
were off in his hands and their bodies were still

flying around the yard because no one had
told them they were dead
yet

First Grade

Miss Logston
said we should
make our
O's
like balloons
she took our
hands in hers
and crushed
our knuckles
like nuts
she made us
draw circles
for hours
round & round
like vultures
circling a
dead donkey

Miss Logston
smelled of
violets
she stuffed
our mouths
with tissue
taped them shut
grabbed us
by the hair
and shook us
senseless

she said
if we talked

out in class
or chewed
gum
or wet our
pants
we would go
to a dark place
where flies
without wings
would crawl over
our open eyes
forever

she
said
we were her
best class
in ten years

she said we
showed
promise

Hit and Run

massive cars
finned like
fish
school quietly
along the
curbs

He ratchets
toward me
on steel skates
the key
swinging from his neck
like a pendulum
or a rope to be
hanged
with

behind his head
the sky
is a cube of sugar
pitted with
shadows

the tar on
the streets
is warm and
chewable
as gum

his face glows
the way
the world

glows
when
you are drunk
or stoned
or in love
beyond
reason

suddenly
he stops
studies his skates
then lifts his head
and hurls himself
toward me again
messenger
of some delinquent
god
laughing and
weaving
between
the implacable
cars

Turkeys

One November
a week before Thanksgiving
the Ohio river froze
and my great uncles
put on their coats
and drove the turkeys
across the ice
to Rosiclare
where they sold them
for enough to buy
my grandmother
a Christmas doll
with blue china eyes

I like to think
of the sound of
two hundred turkey feet
running across to Illinois
on their way
to the platter
the scrape of their nails
and my great uncles
in their homespun leggings
calling out gee and haw and git
to them as if they
were mules

I like to think of the Ohio
at that moment
the clear cold sky
the green river sleeping
under the ice

before the land got stripped
and the farm got sold
and the water turned the color
of whiskey
and all the uncles
lay down
and never got up again

I like to think of the world
before some genius invented
turkeys with pop-up plastic
thermometers
in their breasts
idiot birds
with no wildness left in them
turkeys that couldn't run the river
to save their souls

L. Tells All

I wanted a man
but they were in
short supply
so when this big white
swan followed me home
and announced
"I Am Zeus, Lord of All Creation,"
I crooked my finger at him
and said
"come here, Bird Boy,
let's give it a try."

at first
I have to admit
it was fun
his soft breast
the excited squawk
the way he beat his wings
frantically
like an umpire gone bad
but basically
it was an act of
desperation

we had nothing in common
his feathers made me sneeze
I was afraid to fly
he was married
(of course
they all are)
and we even had religious differences

what can I say?

and then there were his other
women
Io, Europa, Semele
(not to mention the
sluttish little pens he picked up
in the park)

we started to have
terrible fights
I called him an overstuffed
pillow and threw seed
in his face
he threatened to migrate
the usual stuff

by spring
we'd both had enough

one night
while we were sitting
in a Greek restaurant
I told the old cob I'd always
be his friend
but I just couldn't handle
interspecies love

(I lied, of course
the truth was
I'd already started to see
a duck
on the side)

My Methodist Grandmother Said

My Methodist
grandmother said
dancing
was adultery
set to music

how right she was

in that sweet sway
breast to breast and
leg to leg
sin comes into its own

if you have never
waltzed
you cannot imagine
the sheer voluptuousness
of it
the light touch
palm to palm
wool and silk
mixed below the waist
your partner's warm breath
on your neck
coming quicker
and quicker
the strength of the man
the yielding of the woman
so incorrect
so atavistic
so unspeakably sweet

he moves toward you
you back away
he pursues you
and with the faintest
pressure
you encourage him
and watch the blood
rush to his face

not a word is spoken
no one sees this
although it's done in public
in full sight of everyone

you touch
and retreat
meet
and touch again
in time to the music
saying yes
no   yes
no   yes
no
yes

you dance
without thinking of your body
in that gentle
rhythmic
careless
almost copulation

one   two   three
one
two   three

the longest
foreplay
in the western
world

Crossing the Lake

A wooden boat
slap of oars
crimson sumac on the
far shore
the child sets out

the long sheet of
water stretches taut
marred only
by ducks

on the dock
the parents
side by side
growing steadily
smaller

as the child
labors
the lake grows larger
the sky turns hard
the wind rises
and something
dark and
finny
slips
beneath
the bow

Part 2: The Californian

Memories of My Own Underdevelopment

Mexico: Sunday, October 6, 1968

I went out to buy lady
fingers chopped
off I imagined from the hands
of the great baked
lady
(I was 23 and proud of my wit)

the street smelled like charcoal
and tortillas
there were yellow puddles
narrow bone
colored sidewalks
whole families returning
from church

in the plaza a crowd had gathered

a student in a white
shirt
was making a speech
Su sangre! he kept crying
Their blood! Their blood!

I could not hear
the rest so I imagined
a few cops with
clubs
a few bloody heads
I decided he was
overwrought
the boy lacks rhetorical skills
I thought

maybe if he ate
the baked lady's head
he'd be smarter

(I was 23 and proud of my wit
I had not heard the news)

I walked on
toward the store
thinking of small things
my own small
life
my ladyfingers

suddenly three
trucks
pulled into the
plaza

Su sangre! cried
the student

the metal doors on
the backs of the trucks
  rolled up

inside were
soldiers

who said nothing

they simply
began to
fire

Citizen of Nowhere

I came here
as one comes
to all good places:
through catastrophe

when the funnel
first bore down
on me
I went mad with
fear

The sky that afternoon
was the color of green
glass rippled
with smoke

I remember the
wind
picking me up
and hurling me
across the yard

the rest is vague
all I know
is that I woke
in a place where
the sun refuses
to stop shining

in front of my
cottage
is a field of
poppies

for three days now
at dusk
I have seen a
woman
moving across the sky
in a glass globe

The Californian

I wander
among them
with dolphins
on my shirt
a visitor
from a
dry land

I come as
an ambassador
from rattlesnake
country
smelling of
digger pines
and the salt
of the
Pacific

I am a describer
of seals and star
thistles
of earthquakes
the late night
jolt
the run for
the door

from March to November
I tell them
we have no rain

I try to conjure
the red
dust for them
but even the air they
breathe is
green

it all comes
tumbling
down
sooner or
later
I tell them
boulders
mud
freeways
the people you
love
they all crack or burn
nothing is permanent

they listen
politely
some even take
notes

I feel like
a small stone age tribe
recently
discovered by
eager
anthropologists

Solo

this is a land
of private imagination
where nothing
rules but
the intemperance
of dreams

last night
as I sat
on the shore
of the lake
behind my house
a woman made
of bones
suddenly rose
from the waves
and began
to sing

when she finished
I found my hands
filled with birds
and
the petals
of flesh-colored
flowers

The Breakfast Nook

the vision comes
twice
the object out of context:
first ducks
that look like snorkelers
black silhouettes
against a void
then at breakfast the next morning
the bowl that is no longer a bowl
but a white sound
swirling into
a depression
of unspeakable depth
the tea
a brown ocean
reflecting eight moons
my hand
a crippled starfish
naked, albino
floating up from the depths
holding a fork that has become
a long shining road
that branches at the end
into four paths
that lead nowhere

the spoon explodes
clicking and ringing:
bell sounds
rain on a tin roof
water beaded on flesh
and metal

domes of water
sliding down the side
of a glass
miniature worlds
distorted and luminous
all the senses systematically
deranged

the reflection is pitted
against the void
where no reflection
is possible

death can only be seen upside down
through a pinhole camera

the cat in the mirror
attacks itself

Santa Teresa Calls Him
(But He Does Not Answer)

as she kneels barefoot
in her cell
her longing
for him becomes
so intense she breaks
her vow of silence

putting her lips
to the basin
she blows
his name
into the water
and lets it circle there
a small boat
on a vast
ocean

the flame
of the half-gutted
candle
trembles

slowly
    slowly
        slowly
            his name expands

until her
loneliness
fills
the entire
room

Mongoosecivique

The young playwright lies on his back with his
hands at his sides his face yellow

as old furniture polish

he counts the tiles in the ceiling 120
the holes in each tile
23

all the colors are wrong   the walls purple
the light bulbs blue   the windows so
black the sun seems in permanent
eclipse   he grows afraid
so to comfort himself he begins to dream
of writing a new play called "Mongoosecivique"
The play will be set in 1957 in a country
he has never lived in
(somewhere tropical & warm or perhaps
a place where the characters can see
the aurora borealis)

the Mongoosecivique will be a car
but the audience won't know that
until Act III

the characters will
speak of it
enigmatically
as if it were a rare
animal or a beautiful young
woman

Mongoosecivique

the young playwright climbs in
adjusts the mirror
and drives off toward a place
where the aurora borealis
streams over the jungle
and all the colors
are finally
right

Rumor Had It We Were Eating Dogs

we walked through
towns where
the buildings looked
like blocks of congealed honey
and ate the hearts of animals
broiled on sticks
by old women
who waved away the gnats
with dirty hands

rumor had it
we were eating
dogs
rumor had it
the president
had been assassinated
in his palace
in the capital city
on the other
side of a mountain of
salt

we hoarded rumors like
pennies
why were all the fountains
dry?
why did the lights go out
at ten?
what was the purple fruit
the children sold
that tasted like
gunpowder and
string?

we heard a German
botanist
had seen a man
turn into a
jaguar

we thought he was
hallucinating
we thought he might be
telling the
truth

there were rumors of
peace
rumors of war
rumors that we were
betraying each
other

day after day
the planes
flew
overhead
but none
of them
ever
landed

Anza-Borrego

black obsidian
stars
that burned out 30 million years ago
a constellation of ghosts
staring at ghosts

the red tail of Scorpio blinking
like the signal light
on a buoy
seen by a ship
too far out to sea to hear
the warning bell

The Mayans Take Back Yucatan

It's the end of an ordinary day:
along the Caribbean coast
black mangrove roots
thick, pulsing and moist
knit the sea to the land;
in the thatched houses near Chetumal
fried beans simmer in iron pots
and the mouths of the children
are slick with hunger

out on the Lagoon of the Seven Colors
near ancient Bacalar
where the Spanish fort
still reeks of conquest and death
moiré patterns suddenly appear out of nowhere
quivering on the purple, violet, pink
mirror of the brackish water
that's the only sign
only those slow circles
moving out from the center of the lagoon
as the earth shudders under them

two thousand miles to the north
the world has ended

the circles on the lagoon
ripple and overlap
lip to lip
like lovers' kisses
crickets pulse
the air cools

an old man throws a net
the sunset is especially beautiful

a few weeks later
they begin to round up the pale ghosts
and repaint the temples
a few rent-a-car agents
are sacrificed
some tourists put to tearing down
the luxury hotels
SUVs with California plates
lie on their sides
along abandoned highways
and empty beer bottles
glitter in the hot sun
the loudest noise at this stage
is the buzzing of flies

in ten years
the cenotes are full of clean water again
the banana-billed toucans
are back
and the fruit bats
have taken over the Hiltons
rare black coral
has reappeared along the coast of Cancun
fat babies doze in the shade

the universe has a new center
a green navel
soft and loose
as a woman's belly after birth

the jungle and the corn
do their old dance together
and butterflies swarm
and multiply

Each morning the Sun God
smacks his lips
comes out of hiding
and climbs back into the sky

Atlas

this country
is
divided
into 4
provinces

to the north
stretch
forests composed
of human
hair

to the south
deserts sanded
with dreams

imports are few
exports unknown

the capital
city appears and
disappears
at random
like a green
snake sliding
through
tall grass

Peninsula de Osa

just before
dawn
I woke
and turned
to look at you

the light was
underwater
glass green
trembling with
suppressed
sun

your chest was level
your arms limp as
lianas
an ant was making its way
slowly across
your forehead
carrying a scrap of leaf
your face was blue

I thought you had
died

I hoped you had died

The Photographer Longs for Something She Can't Define

her walls are hung
with cross-sections of eternity:
    a line of Indian women
    staggering under baskets of coal
    a Nigerian mother holding a child
    frail as a paper kite
    two young girls from the dry lands
    of northeast Brazil
    dressed in white silk and angel wings
    a Tarascan wedding
    showing the groom's mother-in-law
    dancing in the bloody skin of a flayed goat

as the photographer
inspects her work
a rustling sound
fills her ears
she taps her fingers on the glass
longing to enter each frame

they wanted love
she gave them light
they wanted bread
she gave them beauty

she decides to take
a new series of photographs:
closed doors
crumbling walls
broken windows
ladders that go nowhere

Witness

there were once beasts called elephants
when one could not get food
the others fed her
they were taken for their tusks
which were made into bracelets and piano keys
and their feet which were made into footstools
the seals were made into hats and coats
the salmon were fished out of the rivers
and eaten
the ostriches were taken for plumes for hats
the giraffes became seat covers

there were once trees
older than our oldest cities
with trunks as thick
as the pillars of temples
near the end people tried to save them
by sitting in the tops
but they were forced down
and the trees became plywood

Swordfish were served in fine homes
on long polished tables
covered with exotic sauces
bones of wild mules were
ground up for glue

Mostly it happened by accident
no one meant to get rid of the frogs
at night they used to sing so loudly
we had to shout over the sound of them

and then one summer they sang softly
and then one summer they stopped singing

the honeybees died of some kind of virus
and then the crops failed
and the fruit trees stopped bearing
and a great silence spread over the fields

small things died
things we hardly noticed:
wild grasses
obscure fish
plants that didn't flower
bacteria
tiny brown birds
a kind of grasshopper that only lived in Africa
a plant that grew high up in a tree in the Amazon
where no human being had ever seen it
a biting gnat that people were glad to see go
clothes moths
a Siberian squirrel
some weeds along the side of the freeway
some silly-looking thing that lived in the sand
that the curlews ate
some tiny green plankton that floated in the sea
that no one knew about

soon only the oldest of us could remember
a time when we woke to the humming of the locusts
when a coyote danced in the sagebrush
a beaver felled a tree

a rhinoceros bathed in the mud
and wild roses bloomed in the ditches beside the roads

on summer evenings
large birds
used to cross the thin golden plate of the sun

in the forests
the whippoorwills sang all night long

The Freedom of High Places

1.

In my dreams
the trees grow again
lace their twigs
into a platform
and bear me up
like a survivor on a raft
toward the splendor of crows
and skies half a century old

they offer me a maple trunk
dripping in the rain
rough beneath my hands
its green seeds
spinning down
like butterflies
and whisper of the freedom
of high places
where the twigs are thin

2.

I have watched them bloom
along the Amazon
in purple, red, pale ivory
and felt their warm breath
rise up and toss my plane
like a kite

I have spoken to them
and learned much:
to move slowly

to exercise patience
to take joy in rain

expect a great silence
they warn me
everywhere we are falling
to the chainsaw
and axe

we leave you with regret
willing you all we have:
our orphaned termites
our displaced birds,
some memory of green
and shelter and shade
our unfinished seductions
our eloquent stumps

Greenhouse

sprouting from freeways
purple and red
nasturtium
overpasses
vines tangled
in your hair

the sweet smell of rot
and silence
broken windows
dust everywhere
piles of soft bones
the coyote howls
and night comes down over L.A.
like a cage

Agapanthus

They blossom
every August
like the stripped
skeletons of
blue
umbrellas

how I hate them
those goddamn
beautiful
merciless
flowers

bring me nettles
or a bouquet
of poison oak
plant brambles
on my
grave

but never
make me sit
in a morning-wet
garden
and listen
to two
blue-eyed men
telling lies
while a dozen
agapanthus
on long
green stems

sway slowly
at my knees
like
cobras
begging for
a kiss

Sycamores

look

the sycamores
that line the road
are a fence
of living flames

behind them
the darkness
keeps flowing
like a slow
river

you ask me
why I am here
who I am
what I have
eaten

I say
packs of white dogs
you
and the traveler
who stops
and turns
to look back
one last time

Part 3: When We Were Your Age

When We Were Your Age

we have told you
our youth
was beautiful
we said we danced
naked in the forest
and lay with one another
in the fields

we have shown you pictures
of ourselves
with our arms
around each other
hair plaited
with flowers
tear gas blossoming
behind us
in great white petals
and on every face
a smile
of perfect conviction

we have decorated
our houses with carved gourds
from Peru
stone jars from Greece
and every time
we dust them
we force you
to listen to us tell you that,
when we were your age,
we put everything we owned
in a backpack

and hitched barefoot
across Brazil
slept with cannibals
lived in caves
ate holy herbs
and learned to levitate

we never mention
the nights of dysentery
and raw fear
friends who shot junk
and walked out windows
idiots who refused
to feed their babies
anything but raw broccoli
and acid

our romantic stories
contain no lice
no death
no 18-year-old soldiers
dying in the mud
no speed freaks
in the next room
breaking furniture
and screaming that devils
are coming out of
the kitchen faucets

in these stories
no one ever walks in on her husband
screwing a stranger

on the living room rug
and no one ever has
to be driven
to the psych ward

instead we take to the streets
like packs of jolly elves
the police beat us
but we don't care
we sing
we prevail
we make heroic speeches
about peace and civil rights
we link arms
we dance
we integrate schools
we walk on water
we stop a war
we bring a president
to his knees

the truth is:
we did all that
but we did it
bleeding
we did it
afraid

Not Like We Knew the Answer

we turned
off the paved
road onto
a dirt track
and walked
beneath spider
webs
slung from
tree to
tree
like
hammocks

the webs were
filled with
tiny
worms

we took it
as an
omen

somewhere
a strum of
insects
hummed us
deaf

cicadas I said
locusts you
replied
we stood toe

to toe
arguing
bitterly

(we've been
underground
for 17
years the
locusts said
is it safe
to come
out
now?)

You Are Making Important Decisions

he put fist holes
in walls
broke lamps
smashed shades
shattered windows
grabbed up a butcher knife
and slashed a chair
to shreds

was the man dangerous?
I didn't know

he slept with a gun
under his pillow
but I didn't know
he took Ecstasy
and looked at me with
the eyes of a lemur
but I still didn't know

sometimes he talked
in different voices:
the old cowboy
the sad child
the demented woman
who reminded me
of someone
I had once cared for
but whose name
I could no longer
remember

sometimes he told me
he was Christ
or a visitor from another
planet
it seemed oddly reasonable
perhaps he *was* Christ
perhaps all of us
were only
visiting

at night
he listened
to rebirthing tapes
the baby sliding down
the vagina
the thumping of the
mother's heart

You are making important
decisions
the voice on the tape
warned
decisions
that will affect
the rest of your life

but I paid no
attention

I was making
no decisions
there with Christ

in my bed
with the alien beside me
with the gun
under the pillow
six inches from
my
head

Instructions For Wrestling With Angels

You meet them in the most unlikely places
so at first you may think
they are not angels at all

But look closely:
their lips are dry
their eyes hot
and their only message
is raw need

the desire of angels
is so completely refined
that it coats their cheeks
like grease
and when they have you
in their grip
they can pull your face
to theirs
as easily as if they had
your soul on runners

the first moment
they touch you
is the most terrifying
you can feel their nails
dig into your shoulders
and smell the despair
on their breath

some will hug you
and burn you with their bodies
others will push you away

and then clutch you suddenly
with sharp clicks
like mousetraps going off
under the bed
still others will lie on top of you
until you forget who you are

but you can always tell
when you are wrestling
with an angel
because just under their flesh
you can feel the rusty
edge of your childhood

as they press you
to the earth
their faces will change
like strips of film
superimposed
you may see your mother
or your father
or an old lover
but whoever it is
it will cause you pain

the angels know this
and will use it against you
never let them take you
at night
never let them catch you
off balance

on their backs you will find
two hard ridges
just below their
shoulder blades
slippery and sharp
as fish scales
where their wings
were once attached

if you want to win
take a deep breath
seize those ridges
and pull the angel close

the only thing it can't bear
is love
relentless love
that grabs
and hangs on

Starting Over

Sometimes it's weather:
the wind green and palpitatious
against a black sky
your house up in the cone
everything suddenly gone
except a mirror and a knife

or it's a flood
that carries you out to sea
burning and hallucinating
in the white slice of the waves

or it can be
one of those small moments
when the brain bows
the hand can't clutch
the heart implodes
and you forget words
like
salt
yellow and
umber

Lynchburg

you are not
walking through this field
of yellow flowers

you are not here
you have never been here
you are making yourself from
moment to moment

the blackberry brambles
are making themselves
the cars on Route 29
are making themselves
the sanctuary oaks are making
themselves

nothing is where you left it
it was never there
your shoes are not where you left them
your lovers are not where you left them
even your heart is not where you left it
a moment ago

the cannonballs buried in the forest
under the alders and buckeye trees
are not the same cannonballs
that General Hunter's boys fired
at General Early's boys
each ball
keeps making itself
and every time it makes itself
something is changed
and something is lost

the Confederate boys made themselves
into grass
and the Yankee boys made themselves
into gravel roads
they made themselves into cold fronts
coming in from the north
and tornadoes
sweeping across from the west
and hurricanes blowing in
from the Gulf
and sycamores
and pines
and red dirt

and the widows of the boys
made themselves
into wild onions
plantain
and dandelions
stumps of old trees
fields of hay
and red gashes in the grass where
the new bypass
is coming through
into kudzu
and clover
white rocks
brick buildings
and small windows
with neat wooden frames
libraries
and spent hunting shells

black cows loose on the road
and they're still remaking themselves
moment by moment
into empty beer cans
and girls with long hair
and trucks carrying packages
and propane

the mules that hauled the cannons
made themselves into creeks
and hot asphalt
and the horses the officers rode
made themselves into railroads
and dogs
churches
and broken plumbing
and rust
and they keep on remaking themselves
like the ragweed
and wild roses
that line the ditches
along Coldwell Road

the birds are
relearning their songs
from moment to moment
the kernels of corn
the leaves of the tobacco plants
the mud in the river
have no duration

on that June day in 1864
when the ones in gray rode in on the train
from Charlottesville
and the ones in blue walked over the rise
everything around them
was dying and being reborn

so the boys
took aim
and made
each other
into deer ticks
and mice
the sweet center
of common white clover
dust on windows
in the stables where
the wealthy girls keep
their horses
distant thunder
crows
and a woman in a green T-shirt
bending down
to pick an armful
of flowers

Walking the Neighborhood

A glow of windows
long empty streets crossed
like resting hands
serene trees
feathered against the sky
a sheet of pale clouds
fish-scaled from horizon
to horizon

inside
great colored jewels
pulse with electric phantoms
that chase one another
in shining cars
that have no substance

these are
the dreams
of men
drunk with greed
compassionless as cats

we have invited them over our threshold
and now they dance
before us
like those great medieval murals
raised in the plague years
where Death leads the way
piping on a flute of bone

Samba

Samba
samba
it's always
been
samba

the ferns
in the window
samba
toward the light

the squash
blossoms in the
garden
samba open
and the cucumber
vines samba
up the wall

in the high grass
the crickets
are singing
samba
and the quail
are in a circle
stamping
their feet

the cabbage moths
samba
and the yellowjackets

samba
and even the snails samba
(very very slowly)

out in the Oort
Cloud
Hale-Bopp is
doing the samba
twitching her
long argon skirts

at the edge
of the universe
at this very
moment
billions of
nameless
galaxies are
sambaing away
from one another
at the speed of
light

back on earth
people samba
to work
and samba home
and their dogs
and cats
samba out
to greet them

lovers
samba
all night long
in samba-happy
beds
and new-born babies
dream of nothing
but samba

even
the dead
samba
into the ground
and samba
back out again
leaving
empty spaces
where the
samba
goes on doing
its own
samba forever

Clutter

Sometimes the weight of living
stamps you flat as
a dime

the unread books
& unpaid bills
the dust &
dead people
email, ivy
rotten pipes

stocks that fell
businesses that went bust
languages you forgot
nights spent
staring at the ceiling
beside closets stuffed with
clothes you can no longer
wear

all those love songs you
wrote that never quite
came together
10 with first lines that showed
a promise of seduction
3 with fair middles

then
confusion

verbs with no
subjects

strange
hairs
in your bathroom sink
the ends splayed like
ropes

Whole Note

she unbinds her braid
again and again

time has turned on her

every moment of her life
has become
an old vinyl record
circling in a single grove

for five days
she doesn't
return calls

messages
stick to her
machine
like small
red flies

viola
cello
violin
the adagio drift of
a dragonfly
on water
slowly drawn under
in a long
glassy scroll

Net Surfing 2:00 A.M.

bleary with coffee
and grief for a friend
who died the day before
I find myself staring at the screen wondering
how many pixels it takes
to make a wood duck
or an island of black frigate birds
mating in the mangroves
their globed orange throat pouches
pulsing with birdly lust

in a space no larger than
two hands spanned
flocks of pink flamingos
are migrating
stick-legged, silly-beaked
bits of egg-laying confetti
left over from the big party
of creation

there's comfort in the sight
of so many birds
here at least
I think
life outruns extinction

once in Cambridge
in the Peabody museum
I came across the last passenger pigeon
ever sighted in America
neatly stuffed
with combed feathers and agate eyes

sitting on a fake limb in a glass case
under a card that informed me
it had been shot
by the Harvard expedition of 1893

Audubon himself
killed to sketch

now
electronic snow geese
by the thousands
swirl over the marshes
of the Central Valley
now in one night
I can see
more cranes and herons
than ever fled south
before the snows of winter

I touch the screen with my fingertips
how cold this tiny window is
that drugs us with perpetual flight
the programmers have recreated paradise
and yet...

I pause, consider, and decide:
strike a key
click the mouse
let myself forget
the crossed out phone number
the returned mail
the name he no longer answers to

the silent woods
the long darkness
the
empty
sky

Part 4: Another Piece of Kansas

Replays

who says life must
progress in a straight line?

turn it aside
haul it back
re-run it
I haven't got the
plot down yet
and the characters
are rebelling

I've forgotten my
friends' faces
I can't remember
where I live
old boyfriends stalk my dreams
clutching diaries written
in Aramaic

the past
drifts out behind me
catching everything at random:
dolphins and grandparents
old cars, pennies
rattles, pins
places that no longer exist
except on faded maps
written before wars
no one wants to remember

given the rate of change
I think I deserve
a few replays

I should be able
to prevent stupid
accidents:
uncut myself
while slicing onions
unslip on the ice
drive my car around the truck,
the wall, the kid on the
bicycle

I should be able
to smooth out my face
go back
to 1968
and buy a 6-bedroom house
for $35,000

I should even be able
to resurrect the dead

I have a lot of things
to tell them
things
I was too busy to say
when they were
alive

Poem for Calling Back the Dead

gather white things
paper and bones
a handful of sugar
a mouthful of salt
your baby teeth
on a white cotton string

go down to the sea
and count the clouds
poured like milk
across the water
pick up bleached wood
and brittle shells
wave foam
crab claws
fine, pale sand

when you have given up
everything
even color
your mother will come
with her hair cut short
and her cheeks glowing
and your father will smile at you
from a stranger's face
and your grandmothers will hand you
a bunch of red poppies

somewhere there will be the sound
of frogs and flutes
and the morning sky will take on
the sheen of old pearls
worn close to the flesh

Don't Start Something You Can't Finish

Time travel is easy
take a good look at anything
but be careful
the holes in a button
can become the mouths
of dead relatives
discussing Harry Truman
sweating and smelling of soap
they lean close to one another
their breath sweet and heavy
flies hover above them
like haloes
Om-buzzing the metal spoon
in your baby hand
into a moon or a silver dollar
or the tin dipper
your lover drank out of
fifty years before
when you were both chopping cotton
for Mr. Delapreux
up to your ankles in red mud
sixteen and both of you
wet as a field
and him grabbing you by the waist
and sinking and sinking
into that soft grass you went
with each other's salt on your tongues
and suddenly you're lions
turning each other over
in the dust
maybe this is a hundred years ago
maybe a thousand

you can't tell
you can smell zebras
—a very sexy scent—
and you lash your long tail
and he opens his great red mouth
to give you a love nip
only the red of his throat
gets loose and swells
and fills up everything
and look out
he's a poppy and so are you
and your passion
is reduced to tossing pollen
at each other's stamens
under a sky so clear
it reminds you of water
which it is, of course,
and now the two of you are fish
nosing around in coral sand
on some godforsaken reef
erecting your fins
and dancing around each other
planting your eggs
and milky white seeds
in little bubbles of mucus
that stick together like balloons
and when you try to stop
the transformations
things only get worse
and now you're some asexual
budding thing
and now you're an *E. coli*

in Leonardo Da Vinci's small intestine
and you're saying
sixteen acts of contrition
and swearing off sex altogether
but it's too late
because your DNA is all unraveling
and replicating
and it feels great
like tongues touching
like that button you were looking at
in the first place
that fatal button
on your jeans
that fatal row of buttons
being undone
ever so slowly
one by one

Lucille

the doctors have made her a swimmer
she complains
as she lifts brown webbed hands
to paddle toward the oxygen tank
that chuffs beside her bed

all the ordinary things in her world
are transformed
there are coral, cuttlefish, and purple caracols
in her carpet
tubes in her nose
a giant kelp forest
where she floats helpless and afraid

she struggles toward the lamp
trying to fight her way
to the surface
my sheets, she cries,
have turned into sharks
how do you expect me to iron them?

the power fails suddenly
neighborhood dogs
bark out great jade and gold
bubbles of warning

when the paramedics arrive
sirens screaming
she objects that the whales
are singing too loudly

don't let me drown!

she begs
as they unhook the tubes
give her a new tank
throw her back in
for the long swim

Blue

One day
suddenly
without warning
everyone in the world
turned blue
not the pale washed-out blue
of a summer sky
or the gray-blue
of old silk
but full turquoise
bright and hard as
a Navajo stone
set in silver

at first
there was mass panic
governments fell
commerce collapsed
immigration officials went
into shock
and were found wandering along
fortified borders
singing snatches of old
Lawrence Welk tunes

on battlefields all across
the planet blue soldiers
ran screaming from each other
no one knew who to shoot
no one knew who to hate
the enemy was suddenly
beatified

gorgeous and familiar
as the palm of one's own
hand

in Brazil
three abandoned children
from a cardboard favela
walked unrecognized
through the biggest shopping
mall in Rio
and were accidentally
presented with promotional balloons

in Berlin
five Turkish families
sat on benches in the Zoo
for most of the afternoon
unnoticed and undisturbed

in Miami
a Haitian cab driver
was inadvertently hired
to teach advanced French
at an exclusive
girls' school

as time passed,
the confusion deepened
landlords had to be sedated
real estate agents were found
curled in the fetal position
around For Sale signs

in Chicago
over 200 loan officers
attending a convention
at the Airport Hilton
suddenly took Jesus as
their Savior

but for lovers
blueness was a gift
the world around them
opened up
blossoming and blossoming
like a great blue cornflower

innocent and strange
they lay in each other's arms
blue lips to blue lips
blue breasts to blue breasts
making long, blue love

and when the blue nights
came down at last
and the blue sunsets
hovered over their beds
their blue laughter could be heard
as soft as silver bells
as they whispered to each other
those magic words:
azure
cobalt
indigo
lobelia
aqua

Ex Voto

at dusk
beyond the vineyards
and lilacs
on the far
purple-flecked
horizon
a narrow path
winds through a grove
of chestnut trees

everything
smells of crushed plums
and Chianti
as if some pagan goddess
is eternally
feasting
eternally braiding violets
into her hair

now
night is arriving
from the east
and the winds are
rising
trailing outrider
clouds
that tremble
between mauve
and orchid

on the path
between the lilacs
and the violet-
drenched night
three women
approach
carrying lanterns
that burn
like
gentian

Every Day I Lose Another Piece of Kansas

standing in a
field
as the wind
folded and
unfolded
around my ears
like the
wings
of a great
transparent
butterfly

hot summers
the sibilant
murmur of the
wheat
a small white
house
set like a block
of salt
against a
darkening
sky

the last sunset I saw:
great swaths
of color
small clouds
scudding south
like a flock
of red birds

I was once
a woman with
a family
they had
faces
and habits
and customs
they called
love

I cannot
imagine
them here
eating
plain food
from plain
white dishes
believing
that when they
die
Jesus will
raise
them up
whole

The Grower of Tomatoes

he's out
in the garden
straw hat
freckles of
shade on
his lips

the man who
loves
everything
even the
weeds

especially the
weeds
the slugs
the diaphanous
moths

tomatoes
so juicy
they change
shape in
his hands

simple earth
with nothing
mixed in
but the spray
from the hose
and an eye
for the sparrows

The Kama Sutra of Kindness: Position Number 3

It's easy to love
through a cold spring
when the poles
of the willows
turn green
pollen falls like
a yellow curtain
and the scent of
Paper Whites
clots
the air

but to love for a lifetime
takes talent

you have to mix yourself
with the strange
beauty of someone
else
wake each morning
for 72,000
mornings in
a row so
breathed and
bound and
tangled
that you can hardly
sort out
your arms
and
legs

you have to
find forgiveness
in everything
even ink stains
and broken
cups

you have be willing to move through
life
together
the way the long
grasses move
in a field
when you careen
blindly toward
the other
side

there's never going to be anything
straight or predictable
about your path
except the
flattening
and the springing
back

you just go on walking for years
hand in hand
waist deep in the weeds
bent slightly forward
like two question
marks
and all the while it

burns
my dear
it burns beautifully above
you
and goes on
burning
like a relentless
sun

Missing Your Mouth

today
I am missing
your mouth
your sweet
dark mouth

(a woman is not
supposed to write
poems
to her husband's
mouth
she is supposed
to write poems
to her lover

but I am
shameless
I say I long
for your mouth
and have longed
for it
every day
for seventeen years

for your mouth
your hands
your wrists
and the simple
hollow
you leave
in our bed)

The Visit

like tiny wrinkled
children
the parents arrive
turn their faces
to the sun
and toddle forward
to be hugged

they move awkwardly
testing the gray linoleum
as if it were a bog

she stumbles
and he catches her
and steadies her
with a tender grace

love has tumbled them
together
like old shoes
and nothing short of death
can sort them out

Fishing And Weaving

in a room
where the windows
are radiant with dust
you sit
with your back to the wall
weaving white cotton

you toss it toward me
and it billows like smoke
rattles like stones
falls like pearls

I'm happy here!
you cry
your words become cloth
each cross-thread a vowel
each long thread a consonant
good
sturdy, tight,
pale
a shroud
not likely to ravel

Notes

1. "Memories of My Own Underdevelopment" is set in a large Mexican city in October of 1968, a few days after the Mexican army and police forces shot and killed hundreds (some say thousands) of high school and college students and workers in Mexico City in the plaza of Tlatelolco. The demonstrators had assembled to protest governmental repression, neglect of the poor, inadequate funding of education, and the armed occupation of the campus of the National Autonomous University of Mexico. The Tlatelolco massacre, which haunted the Mexican imagination for decades, took place just before Mexico hosted the Olympic games.

2. *Mongoosecivique*
In 1955, the Ford Motor Company commissioned Marianne Moore to make up names for their latest model. Her suggestions included: *The Utopian Turtletop*, *The Intelligent Whale*, and *Moongoose Civique*. Ford rejected all the names Moore sent them and called their new car The Edsel.

About the Author

MARY MACKEY was born in Indianapolis, Indiana. After receiving a B.A. from Harvard, she attended the University of Michigan where she received a Ph.D. in Comparative Literature. She is the author of four previous collections of poetry, including *The Dear Dance of Eros*; one experimental novella, *Immersion*, and ten novels, including *A Grand Passion*, *Season of Shadows*, and *The Year the Horses Came*. Her literary works have  been translated into eleven foreign languages including Japanese, Hebrew, Greek, and Finnish. Mackey has lectured at Harvard and the Smithsonian. She is past president of the West Coast branch of PEN, a Fellow of the Virginia Center for the Creative Arts, and Professor of English and Writer-in-Residence at California State University, Sacramento, where she teaches creative writing and film. A member of the Writers Guild of America, West, she wrote the screenplay for the award-winning feature *Silence*. At present, she is co-writing film scripts with Hollywood director Renée De Palma. More information about her can be found at www.marymacky.com.

PHOTO: ANGUS WRIGHT

GOSSIP, Thomas Fink
ARBOR VITAE, Jane Augustine
BETWEEN EARTH AND SKY, Sandy McIntosh
THE POND AT CAPE MAY POINT, Fred Caruso and Burt Kimmelman
THE BEE FLIES IN MAY, Stephen Paul Miller
MAHREM: THINGS MEN SHOULD DO FOR MEN, Edward Foster
REPRODUCTIONS OF THE EMPTY FLAGPOLE, Eileen R. Tabios
DRAWING ON THE WALL, Harriet Zinnes
SERIOUS PINK, Sharon Dolin
BIRDS OF SORROW AND JOY: NEW AND SELECTED POEMS,
    1970–2000, Madeline Tiger
ORIGINAL GREEN, Patricia Carlin
SHARP GOLDEN THORN, Chard deNiord
HOUSE AND HOME, Rochelle Ratner
MIRAGE, Basil King
NATURAL DEFENSES, Susan Terris
BRYCE PASSAGE, Daniel Morris
ONE THOUSAND YEARS, Corinne Robins
IMPERFECT FIT, Martha King
AFTER TAXES, Thomas Fink
NIGHT LIGHTS, Jane Augustine
SOMEHOW, Burt Kimmelman
WATERMARK, Jacquelyn Pope
SKINNY EIGHTH AVENUE, Stephen Paul Miller
THE AFTER-DEATH HISTORY OF MY MOTHER, Sandy McIntosh
WHITHER NONSTOPPING, Harriet Zinnes
I TAKE THEE, ENGLISH, FOR MY BELOVED, Eileen R. Tabios
THE GOOD CITY, Sharon Olinka
UNDER THE WANDERER'S STAR, Sigman Byrd
WHAT HE OUGHT TO KNOW: NEW AND SELECTED POEMS,
    Ed Foster

Marsh Hawk Press is a juried collective committed to publishing poetry, especially to poetry with an affinity to the visual arts.

Artistic Advisory Board: Toi Derricotte, Denise Duhamel, Marilyn Hacker, Allan Kornblum, Maria Mazzioti Gillan, Alicia Ostriker, David Shapiro, Nathaniel Tarn, Anne Waldman, and John Yau.

For more information, please go to: http://www.marshhawkpress.org.